Our Sick Pets

by Jessica Quilty

Scott Foresman
is an imprint of

Glenview, Illinois • Boston, Massachusetts • Mesa, Arizona
Shoreview, Minnesota • Upper Saddle River, New Jersey

Here is Pip.
She is sick.

Here is Bix.

He is sick.

Here is Vin.

He is sick.

5

Here is the vet.
She can fix Pip, Bix,
and Vin.

Here is Tim.
What can he do?
Tim can take Vin back.

How to Be a Vet!

Some people who like science and animals want to become vets. People go to school for many years to be vets. There are special schools that teach how to be a doctor for animals. There are thousands of vets in the United States!

8